This book is dedicated to those who continue to sing to me

My maternal great-great grandmother: Driscilla Condor
My paternal great grandparents: James George Roberts & Agnes Roberts
My maternal great grandparents: Joseph Hutton & Harriet Lewis Hutton,
My maternal & paternal grandparents: Dora Aletha Hutton Francis &
Nathaniel Noel, Iris Roberts & Moses Mendes
My parents: Cleopatrilla Noel Roberts, Joseph (Maurice Mendes) Roberts

To those who will continue the songs
My brothers & sisters, nieces & nephews

Special Thanks to those who have supported my writing
Tanya Saunders, Cyril Husbands, Cresswell, Bill Sheasgreen, Malve Slo-
cum Burns, Kadija George, Pat Griffin, Jessica & Eric Huntley, Fishbone
Writers: Samia, Joe, Sue, & Judith

PREFACE

My Grandmother Sings To Me is remarkable not least because of the sheer size of Maureen Roberts's first published collection – fifty nine poems - but also the range and breadth of their explorations and concerns: from musings on love, the *everydayness* of everyday life, the burgeoning awareness of a child, new to England, of the subtle ways that the society chips away at her self-worth and her skin, through to explorations of heritage, progeny, journey and non/belonging.

Heritage and memory, as the title of the book suggests, figure strongly especially in the early part of this work. Here we find (again as the title suggests) one of the abiding themes of contemporary women authors, writing themselves out of the 20th century and into the 21st: the idea of generational continuity, of cultural and aesthetic relay. An acknowledgement and celebration of the silver line that connects generations of Caribbean women (*My grandmother sings to me/ her song entwined with the voice of my mother*) despite being separated by an Atlantic that still heaves with the traumas of a remembered past.

It is a past which Roberts seems to suggest (as in the poem *The Old Cliché*) is still very much present, and with us today. One wonders how much of that past, for example, has shaped the attitude of a Brixton male in search of his *'African queen'* who passes her everyday on the streets but never sees her?

It is this interface between past and present - the living and the lived - that gives this book so much of its resonance. Roberts seems to suggest also, that memory, like blood, can be inherited.

These poems feel as though they are composed at times when the writer withdraws in order to disengage meaning out of her observations in any given day. Two of the many poems that are illustrative of this are *Sun Gods* and *An Ethiopian Woman on the Train to Luton*. It's an impression that seems to be supported by the author's own illustrations in this book.

These poems, even when they draw on the resources of the 'grandmother' language, (Eastern Caribbean Creole) are never strident. They never fall back on verbal pyrotechnics for effect. What we have here is a careful deployment of craft to arrive at meaning.

This is a book that will last and last.

Jacob Ross

CONTENTS

Echoes

THE BEGINNING......8

SHE IS NOT HERE......9

REMEMBERING......10

GRANDMA SWEEPS......11

THE OCEAN......12

DO THEY KNOW HOW GOOD LIFE IS?......13

MY GRANDMOTHER'S CHILD......15

MY GRANDMOTHER SINGS TO ME......17

POLISHED SILVER......19

THE JETTY......21

FOOD FILE......22

SUN GODS......23

A FAREWELL SONG......27

MERLINA......31

SOMEONE ELSE......32

BRUSHING ASIDE SPIDER WEBS......34

LEAVING......35

Margins

THE WAY WE WERE......37

FRESH MORNINGS......43

COME LET US TALK......45

THIS PATCH IS MINE......50

THE LONG GONE WOMAN......52

SNOW QUEEN......55

THE ETHIOPIAN WOMAN ON THE TRAIN TO LUTON......57

THE CAYMANIAN ARTIST IN MANHATTAN......58

OLD CLICHE......59

EYE TO EYE......60

Transience

TURN DOWN THE DAWN 62
MORNING 63
I'M SITTING HERE AWHILE 64
MORNING CHORES 65
CAYMAN SCHOOL DAY 66
AFTERNOON CLASS 67
TIME IS SHORT 68
AMRYL 69
A JAR OF WORMS 70
LIKE WATER 72
NOT COFFEE SPOONS 73
BOB DYLAN SANG 75
CAYUGA LAKE 76
SICK DAY 77
WEST BAY LOVE SONG 78
CARIBBEAN SUNSET FALLS 80
TIME FLIES 81
CAYMAN KAI LOVE SONG 82
NIGHT LINGERS 83
MELLIFLUOUS 84

Embrace

THE WALL 86
TWELVE 89
PEOPLE 91
THE RETREAT 93
PACING TIGERS 95

Sentience

DON'T TALK TO ME OF LOVE 98
THOUSANDS MADE 99
CUBAN STORM 100
LITTLE MAN 103
LET MUSIC FLY 105
GREEN MOON 107
BACK HOME 108
END SONG 109
ACKNOWLEDGEMENTS 111

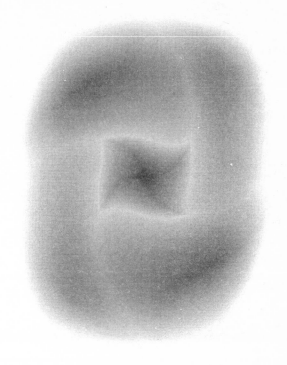

Echoes

THE BEGINNING

...and I can smell you
deep inside my brain
for you are impulse
scattered through and through my frame...

SHE IS NOT HERE

She is not here. I am here
I hear her words as people remember her
She was a baker of bread and cake, an interpreter of dreams
She is not here. I am here.

I breathe her sun and sea.
My heart lives here, never goes away
in any other place, I am heart less.
She is not here. I am here.

REMEMBERING

Memory
Remember me to...
Reminding me of...

When you were a young woman
skin smooth, and baby fresh, what was the world like?

Can I remember through your memory?
Through the memory of your voice telling a story?

Sun black, sun smooth am I
Soon I will blend into this land.
Walk hills unbound by time
swim on the bottom of oceans and not return.

They say the first group of Africans brought to this land
flew back to Africa

I have flown to Africa and flown here.
I retain a memory of a journey on foot through Africa,
through Grenada, it is all one.
A memory snagged on time.

GRANDMA SWEEPS

Grandma sweeps, shooing chickens, feeding them,
like she feeds us, her England grand children.
"What all you does eat, cornflakes?" and we laugh
asking for green bananas, salt fish and black sage tea.
She gives us coffee, scrambled eggs and fresh baked bread.
It is our duty to be English and show some kind of improvement.
After all you can't have lived in England all these years
and come back eating green bananas.

THE OCEAN

The ocean misses us, I know
It waits with a restless simmering calm,
building waves to dash against pebbles,
to smooth shattered glass,
hungry to anoint our lips with salt,
sting our eyes.

It sits moon-blue, brooding at dusk
anticipating star glazed nights without us.

When sun warm waves
achieve fresh turquoise clear,
seagulls sit and wait
bobbing in watery armchairs

The ocean misses us, I know
but has no pen to write,
flings glassy droplets of spray on dry land,
drums endless moon pulled rhythms.
We are so far away, listening but barely hear.
Traffic rumbles in our distant ears.

We sit night-blue brooding at dusk;
eyes glazed watching distant stars
and ocean dreaming.

DO THEY KNOW HOW GOOD LIFE IS?

Do they know how good life is?
The men and boys who cycle the jetty,
riding out to meet the ocean
limitless, horizon ahead of them
coconut and palm behind
suspended in nutmeg scented air.
Do they know how lucky they are?
As the loud laughter
bounces off concrete jetty
tumbles through sea salt spray
skips through palm fronds,
falling starlight
shimmering in ocean waves,
Island children, Cassandra and Ariel
play here, touched by gods.

MY GRANDMOTHER'S CHILD

My grandmother loves children
I am my grandmother's child.
Love and bond forged before I was five
I played on this hill, over looking this bay,
these sunsets are mine.
The sound of the sea rises and falls in my blood.
My lungs were opened in the salt of this air.
These trees, tamarind, mango, coconut, calabash and lime
swayed with my first faltering steps.
The hillside rang with my cries
and delighted in my first words.
The crabs hid deep in their holes from my prying sticks.
The rabbits were soft to my touch.
A hill was no barrier to my scrambling journeys to meet the sea.
Here I was loved.
Memory clear as a river runs through my heart.

MY GRANDMOTHER SINGS TO ME

My grandmother sings to me
her song entwined with the voice of my mother.
Our mother sang when the daylight dawned
on awakening from the womb
she sang the songs of the newly born,
an off key wailing that sentences parents to servitude.

The crystal rivers, turquoise waters of an island
flowed and ebbed to her voice.
Her song settled over rock stone, river stone
Benago Bay, Gouyave Bay, and Grand Anse.

She sang to her grandmother, Harriet
and cooled the hot macadam road
that burned bare feet as they walked
over the l'anse.

Her song lies in the embroidered pillowcases
of Miss. Doris who taught her to sew
It lay warm in the oven-baked bread
of her mother.

Her song was ground into cinnamon
with pestle and mortar
sliced into chipped coconuts of sugar cakes
bubbled with boiled yam, fig, dasheen

stewed with damsons, boiled slowly
with guava jelly, guava cheese.
Flattened into cakes of farine.

This song sliced into the belly of jacks
shed their iridescent scales
made split pea soup overflowing with dumplings,
ground corn to make asham,
lighted oil lamps as the sun's rays
slipped from the swaying horizon.

When ocean weary the children of Noah
arrived in an inhospitable land
her song grew faint
floated to the clouds
melted into the screeching of gulls.

Her melodies searching for solace
were resurrected between cold pews
and life giving Sunday morning sermons

Each child borne added harmony to her song
six children for ever singing at the hem of her skirt
demanding from her the world
which she gave.

Our songs will never leave you
and yours will not leave us.
My grandmother sings to you
as she sings to me
And you my mother have sung to me
as I now sing to you.

POLISHED SILVER

I wake and sleep with you
announce your arrivals and departures
have soothed your anxiety by my touch

the echo of my voice precedes your destiny
we are bound to her forever by my presence
patterns etched at my birth have been absorbed by you

I am worn smooth by both your journeys
my light rivals the moon when you are well
I turn black when you are ill

I have kneaded dough with you both
I walked to market with her covered in sweat

I walk through shopping malls with you

she fed chickens goats and pigs
sorted nutmeg, chopped wood, pounded cinnamon
the fine dust of her labours I retain within me

You talk to students, use computers
we keep her in our hearts
As I will keep you in mine

I carry the sum of all your days within me
Not only do I encircle your wrist
I encircle your life

THE JETTY

The little boys are hurling themselves off the jetty in Gouyave
They splash and splish, brown bodies naked,
Glistening with sun, sea and salt
They are every tumbling shade of brown
A sienna rainbow web of skinny legs, spindly arms, brave hearts.

"Watch me Sailor, watch me. Sailor watch me, watch me."

They frog jump, pelican dive into clear water,
too close to the rocks lining this bay.
Sailor watches, his rasta locks shaking as he laughs.

"Go further down," he shouts, "Don't jump from there."

"Watch me Sailor, watch me. Sailor watch me, watch me."

Splish, splosh, sun-baked bodies jump,
their shrieks of delight sing through sun clear air.
Sing into salt drenched memory.

"Watch me Sailor, watch me. Sailor watch me, watch me."

FOOD FILE

I've tried foie gras,
      boursin
           coq au vin,
                steak and kidney pudding? Mille-feuille, haggis,
                        guinness, sauerkraut, pecan pie,
                            shepherd's pie, scotch eggs,
                          apple pie with nutmegs,
                    but, nothing quite compares to
            saltfish,
          with or without ackee,
       run-down, oil-down, souse,
    coo-coo, okra, pelau, pilau,   curry goat, fry fish, bami,
                fish broth, mauby,
                  sorrel, dumplings,

                  molasses
                      on coconut,

              boiled yam, farin, fish cakes,
              saltfish cakes, bakes,
         fry chicken, bake yam,
    All too good to talk about.   Let's nyam.

SUN GODS

The boys are on the beach again
tall, dark and lean
their oiled bodies glide between residents and visitors.
Healthy, home grown boys, spawned from surf, sand and sea.
Flexing their muscles; laughing out loud.
The sun's rays flash a rainbow
from their bone white teeth.
Sun gods,
they flex their sun-filled muscles
and laugh and wait;
occasionally sipping a beer,
red stripe, carib, heineken.

Sun and sand psychologists they pick
up each distressed damsel vibration
long before the sender is aware of transmitting.
They home in, slowly, gently,
hovering on the edges of her conscious mind.

The victims succumb, willingly,
to the honey flowing from lips and eyes.
As the sun burns into bare skin
oil is rubbed into red backs, sides,
thighs, calves, toes.
from shoulder and lashes, salt spray
is licked with a warm tongue.

Later they'll dance
slow
cheek to cheek
heart to chest.

The secret cornucopia of island life now
opens up to the woman.
The westerner's desire for knowledge
will lead her down dirt track roads
to visit with the explorer's eyes,
dog city, monkey town and more.
She will make love to the sound of torrential rain
pounding on a galvanised roof.
Eat marinated conch and drink fish tea.
In his arms she will be loved.
Princess of the islands
more beautiful than Nefertiti,
more favoured than Sheba's queen.

Too soon it is time to go,
to trade sarong and thong sandals
for suit and sweaters.
She can not bear to leave him.
She will buy him a ticket
and he will promise to be with her
in a couple of weeks, a month at most.
She leaves with new found radiance and beauty.
The boys are on the beach again

Echoes

Tall, dark, lean bodies
gleaming with oil, a gold chain,
a thick gold bracelet
bought with the price of tickets to
snowy destinations.

A FAREWELL SONG

White clouds, grey streaked
       her early morning hair
              Waiting to be combed by sunrays
                  parting locks of clouds.
Her frock swirling coconut branches,
       lifting up high in the early morning breeze
           settling around her knees
              in the glassy translucence
                 of aqua seas.

Came to find you
       speaking soft to me like these island whispers
           and you were gone.
           Rising up with a pre-dawn breeze
              you decided not to wait
                ten years was too long

Though I might have come sooner
       but couldn't with you gone.

       Came to find you
           baby, child, teenager and adult as I am
             but couldn't with you gone.

       Look it rains, sweet smelling, soft and warm
           like your cheeks on my face.

I have grown my hair long for you
    the way you would prefer it.
        I will wear it in plaits
            but who will plait it?

    I have come, as I came before, on other visits.
        I am well, mammy, daddy, all the children
            everyone is well and send their love.

        Came to see you but you had gone away.
        Left no address.

    Pulling your skirt up
        placing it between your knees you said,
            "it's time to go. After all I'm weary
        I've walked countless steps to Douglastan and back.
            I've sifted and sorted enough nutmeg.
    I've carried enough feed for Nan, the goat and those damn
rabbits.
        Baked enough bread, bun and coconut tart.
        It's time to rest."
            Your filmy eyes peering into another sunset
              across the bay at Gouyave, Benago 1

The flowers are gone.
    The stubborn rose that climbed over the door
        The pots filled with flowering plants.
        The black sage, the thyme.

Echoes

The fruit trees, except the tamarind, mango and lime,
All gone. What without you could survive?
I came to find you and you were gone.

"Child, life goes on."

Last time I saw you the sadness in your eyes, as if you knew
you would not wait for my return
I can't remember saying goodbye
I'm searching my memory to find your words
to find your smile.

I'm waiting for your visit in a dream
clearer than cinematic film
I know you'll come when time is right
breathing a soft
"Bon dieu, eh eh, oui papa."
And you'll smile
seeing the little girl of four or five

the child who knew better than to leave you behind
to go to England.
The child who wept and screamed

"Dada, Dada, come for me Dada, come for me. Don't go".

"but you going to England, to you mammy."

And I was gone.

Black child, calypso in my soul,
　　　red earth dance pounded into the soles of my feet.
　　　so many partings.

I had a dream one time that I a skinny black child
　　was walking across dry, sun-cracked savannah
　　　　with my nomad family. Old men with sticks,
　　　　　dogs with strange wolf hound heads,
　　　　　　high arching backs and sparse, shaggy coats

looking for our next home
　　looking for home
　　　　while fierce dogs barked at us.

Who will interpret my dreams?
　　Who can know without the gift?
　　　　I only knew I was ancestral dreaming.

And where are you to tell me why and how?
　　And what can I, a mere child,
　　　　know of the purpose of adults and this world?
　　　　　Who am I and what do I know at the last?
　　　　　　Except that this final parting
　　　　　　　　hurts.

MERLINA

Merlina came like some ancient prophet
burnt molasses black skin
rain drop bright eyes
bark strong, cricket agile
quicker than a mosquito
bobbing and weaving like the boats alongside the pier
Merlina came
skinny like a string bean
smelling of rum
brimming with aboriginal secrets
a ripe mango full and ready to burst.
She came to tell me of my grandmother's death
her last hours
the washing and the dressing of her
the bottle of rum under the bed
the money under the mattress
who took what.
Who else could my grandmother send?
She delivered her message and was gone.
The price of her next glass of rum
safe in a non-existent bosom.

SOMEONE ELSE

Someone else lies on the pillows now
walks up the spiral staircase,
opens wide the sliding doors,
allows the serene evening breeze
its ritual dance around the central pillar.

The towels slung carelessly
hang forlorn over cane furniture
but belong to another now.
Perhaps the plants survive
curling tendrils forcing their way
through breeze block stones.

Someone else turns on the shower.
Splashing cold water on those bare white tiles.
Perhaps they hear the baby cry,
and the tapping of crab's claws
against glass doors at night.

Someone else chases the mint green lizards
across the brown tiled floors
battles with maroon dark cockroaches
and encourages fireflies to shine
in the round house on West Bay Road.

Echoes

Someone else sweeps away the water
after each storm.
Airs the cupboards to prevent mildew.
Gathers friends together to talk,
eating and drinking late in the comfort of night.

And when the Nor'wester blows
It is that stranger who closes all the doors.

BRUSHING ASIDE SPIDER WEBS

Breeze ripples through our home,

a scattering of dust blowing

through surf and waves

Even on Sunday the sound

A cousin chips away rust on a truck;
frame.
We will do the same to this house.
food.
Loud squawking on the steps...

so raucously, so out of tune?

Waves mount a slap-hearted,

with each breath we take.

a whispering trail through this old house...

This is the final goodbye.

fills out mismatched curtains.
We came, now go,

in our wake...
The sun bounces hymns

stirring long forgotten memories

of hammer on steel.

welding new material to an old

Rhianna's cat returns, looking for

What bird could sing

A chick that lost its way.

crescendo, while we sleep,

We sweep the dust that leaves

LEAVING

In my head I am always leaving
measuring the time
casting and trawling through my mind
for what will allow me to stay.

I am always leaving
disappearing into foreign lands.
I could be happy here
watching the sunsets

cradled and caressed by this breeze
burnt black by this sun.
I could be happy here.
But I am always leaving.

THE WAY WE WERE

They thought we did not speak English.
Our words lilted up to grey skies,
fell in sweet cadences to our ears only.
We learned that a bloomer was bread
not knickers
We learned to count shillings and pence
not dollars and cents
which made more sense.
Had to wait for metric
before we could give up
twenty shillings to the pound
forget three pence and six pence
half a crown, ten shilling notes,
silver three penny pieces.

The woman in the bread shop
stole my silver three penny piece
told me it was not six pence
sent me home to get another
three pennies
before she would hand over
my large white, sliced, loaf
small, brown, hovis,
unsliced of course.
Stood waiting in the green grocers
to buy Irish potatoes
for West Indian soup.
They thought I was too young
to understand them.

They did not understand us.
Stood waiting
while the greengrocer
and his headscarfed customer
discussed us.
"They are so ugly."
They said. Listened
to a whole conversation on how
ugly we were, but then
they looked at me standing
patiently waiting for
my turn to buy Irish potatoes
which mammy said
they called King Edward's in England.
"At least she's pretty" they,
the ugly ones said
and lo and behold
they were talking about me
assuming still
that I did not speak English.
Got my potatoes
went to the butchers
joined another queue.
They are still discussing us.
Local butcher to customer
"when they come in they
always reject the first thing
I put my hands on
So, I always pick up
the good meat first."
Told my mammy what I had heard

got good meat
from that butcher from then on.

It took a long time for them
to see us
We all looked alike after all.
Funny that
because
they all looked the same to me then,
Sometimes even now.

Mother sent us to dancing school
learned tap, ballet and
something called modern.
She sewed elastic in my dancing shoes
in the late evenings
while listening to the radio
sitting in the big armchair
with the rose patterned stretch covers.
She bought me the little, yellow,
pleated, dancing skirt
the purple, hand knitted, cross-over cardigan,
the leotard, the tights,
and I danced
but crippled by shyness
never showed my freestyle pieces
to the rest of the class
when asked.
Watched theirs
Did not mind demonstrating
my perfect, natural turn out

or a particularly high grand jeté.

At our annual party, won a prize
went to get it
was not allowed to pick what I wanted
like everyone else had.
Ballet mistress
thrust into my hand
the cheapest thing on the table
a plastic make up bag.
Looked into her eyes.
Learned,
the meaning of prejudice
Learned,
a smile can tell lies.

My father would arrive each month
to pay for all our lessons
His children
never counted out shillings and pennies
each week like the other kids.
He was always, proud, smiling
magnanimous, wealthy seeming.
He did not see, did not understand
that she, the ballet mistress
hated us, my sisters and me
especially when, precisely because
he took crisp, pound notes from
his pocket and paid her.

She made us take extra ballet lessons

to prepare for exams, which we never took
for which, we were never entered.

Took piano lessons
from an elderly, smooth-cheeked
old, English lady who loved music, ergo life
My mother, now mum and mummy
when I talked about her
still mammy when I talked to her
always wondered why
the piano teacher did not marry.
My youth told me
she had better things to do with her life.

The piano teacher pushed silver, grey angel's hair
from her face and talked to me
prepared me for exams
which I took.
Knew that I understood English
better than most.
Gave me warm Ribena before
I entered cold exam rooms
fingers stiff with fear
vocal chords contracted with the curse
of shyness
made me skip grade I
go straight to grade II
she always knew what I could do.
Taught me new ways to look at life,
but I realised when she
gave me and my sister
a lift home one day

she checked out our house
the size, the type, the street.
This saddened me
because
I knew then
that even if you beat race
that still leaves class.

FRESH MORNINGS

He used to hold a balloon on a string
hit it gently and watch it float back to him.
He spun seeds which sailed
through the air
like helicopters.
Licked sherbet from the palm of his hands.
Stroked "Piggy" the guinea pig with love.
Cradled his younger brother in his arms.
Thought watercress was flowers,
"Pass the flowers", he said
pointing to the salad bowl.
He played marbles against walls
and over drainage gratings.
Sang, "The big ship sailed on the
alley, alley O."
Ran home crying
inconsolable
when someone stole his football boots.
Fresh mornings gave way to dark waters.
When white shirt, dark suit
bright tie, eluded him,
he hung out on street corners
snatched a handbag or two
and ran like the wind.
Washed cars for a while;
picked up a few items

from the supermarket.
Forgot to pay.
Found a couple of cordless phones,
parked by the side of the road.
Saw a child's balloon floating away
reached out, pulled it back to him
watched the child walk away.
Waited for the balloon
to float back to him.
Didn't know why.

COME LET US TALK

Come let us talk
Come let us talk
Come let us talk
About things
You know, you and me you and we
We've been talking for a long long time.

Let's talk about how
You plucked us away
From our African tribe and our ancestry
Denied us a culture
Denied us a language
Totally, completely, reshaped our future
Packed us in a ship
Like peas in a tin can, peas in a tin can

Come le' we talk
Come le' we talk
Come le' we talk
About things..

Let's talk about what we both expect
Let's try to give each other a little respect
Perhaps then you will come to understand
That where you're leading
Is not where we're going

Come let us talk
Come let us talk
Come let us talk
About things

When our parents first came to the motherland
They didn't come to stay, just came to lend a hand
Wanted a little money to go home, buy land
Found themselves working in factories night and day
Ten shillings a week, food and rent to pay
Still they sent a little money back home each week

They worked all the hours God could send
Got up early in the morning, went to bed well after ten
They didn't come to stay, just came to lend a hand
They had it all planned, they had it all planned
They didn't come to stay, just came to lend a hand
Wanted some money to buy a piece of land

Come let us talk
Come let us talk
Come let us talk
About things

Some sent for their daughters, some for their sons
They sent for mothers, husbands and wives
Brothers and sisters whether one or five.

'le we make some money, but we must stick to we plan
When we make some money we can go home, buy land'

Come le' we talk
Come le' we talk
Come le' we talk
About things

So many of them all living in a room
Hair pressing, food cooking, clothes washing
Paraffin heater smelling and life living.

The fogs were thick, the winters cold
They had to spend money on heavy over coats.
Once in a while when they felt most alone
Grandma sent a box all the way from home.

Ground provisions, yam, cassava, dasheen
sweet potatoes, green bananas, ripe plaintain
bush tea, thyme, ferrol, limacol,
farin, white rum and tamarind balls.

Saltfish, herrings, mackerel and jacks
sugar cane wrapped in flour sacks
vanilla, nutmeg parched corn and mace,
All nectar in a land that was foreign and strange
A little piece of balm to ease a lot of pain.

Come le' we talk
Come le' we talk
Come le' we talk
About things..

They didn't come to stay
They had it all planned
Wanted some money to buy a piece of land

In autumn was rain, in winter was snow
spring was well, spring...just so so
But the living was fine in the summer time
they gathered together, shared a bottle of rum
and talked 'ole talk all night long.
Talked about moon light brighter than day
talked about rivers, streams and bays
talked about loupgaroo and men who deal
about cutting cane and feeding pigs
about washing in rivers
swimming in the sea
catching land crab
and eating lambie
and Sunday was church and drinking cocoa tea.

Come le' we talk
Come le' we talk
Come le' we talk
About things.

You know you and me you and we
We'll be talking for a long, long time.

THIS PATCH IS MINE

Insects have scattered themselves
over this heaving mass of warm vomit
left by a homeless alcoholic
marking his territory
as dogs mark lamp posts

"this patch is mine...
avoid... avoid..."

the putrid stench
reels up from slimy pavement
causes eyes to avert
locks into nostrils
and assaults the mind

"this patch is mine..."

so we avoid
step over vomit
step over man
deny... deny...

shudder in disgust
at what should make us cry.

THE LONG GONE WOMAN

I

"Welcome, welcome, our longlost brothers&sisters."

Wrapped in the cadences of smiles
familiar rests indelible in your eyes.

I have been a long gone woman from these shores.
Yet my heartbeat picks up the Serakunda rhythms
swirling in red dust devils
seeking to cover my sandaled toes.

Spun thread to its hook
a warm breeze weaves me
back into the delicate fabric of belonging
creates the scratching catch in the throat
the suspicion of tears.

We, *noplacetocallhome* people walk easy here
comfortable in this daytime dreaming,
sun shimmering skin and warm air breathing,
touching trees whose bark might hold
the imprint of family strangers. You,
the ones who left, the ones we do not know.
Long gone.

II

You don't know about Marlene?
Girl, she long gone, mad as a hatter
Madder than March Hare. It sad oui,
but is so life is.

She talking to me saner than judge
just the other day, not long,
then in Brixton yesterday.
waiting for that never come 250 bus
I see her, but it don't look like her.

People can change, oui
hardly a scrap of hair on the girl head.
Like she *shaveoffsome&pullout* the rest,
she *shaveoffsome&pullout* the rest,
and she standing at the bus stop stripping,
she standing at the bus stop stripping
Her two breasts *expose&swinging*
Two breasts *expose&swinging.*

Everybody pretending they not looking
but I look and I see she was crying, just crying.

III

"I'll call you tomorrow."
But I was long gone
having grown tired of waiting for *tomorrowcallls*
Inanhourcalls, laterintheweekcalls
All those never never calls.

In this aeroplane, another aeroplane
Flying away from broken promises
I wonder why Extra Terrestrials can phone home
But not earthlings.

Used to wait for big promises to be broken
now I leave after the small ones
why multiply the pain?

Three strikes, you're out of my field of dreams
and I'm away to new adventures, new *sights&scenes*
Yet, still open to encounters of the third kind
spellbound and wishing for fairy tale endings.

Don't look for me five minutes after the hour
when spells are broken. It is the hurting hour.
While you were making plans, I was long gone.

SNOW QUEEN

Skulking along icy edges of street corners
has become your life
Chasing shadows in the night
Stalagmites grow through your feet
The snow queen froze your body
took your life.

Diamonds, opals, sapphires, malachite
I could have understood
but this?

The snow queen stole your mind
then iced your heart
Now locked away in her winter palace
She feeds you on her grey-white rocks.

Diamonds, opals, sapphires, malachite
I could have understood
but this?

The comfort of the foetal fold
Does not protect against her cold
Cowrie shells replaced your eyes
The snow queen turned your heart to ice
now, all your promises are just lies.

Diamonds, opals, sapphires, malachite
I could have understood
but this?

Warm tears feed grief
Do not provoke the thaw of spring
Within, without, without, within
Do not melt a single shard of icy heart
The snow queen stole you, each and every part.

Diamonds, opals, sapphires, malachite
I could have understood
but this?

THE ETHIOPIAN WOMAN ON THE TRAIN TO LUTON

Slender like thin reeds in May,
hair wisping in January's cold gray.
Cream wool coat folds, belts, bulks
her frame. Frail Ethiopian woman
barely able to step up to the train.

We catch her when she sways
before she falls and breaks
scattering cream wool coated marbles
on the platform, rolling down the tracks,
catch, her, catch her quick, mind her back!

Next to him she sits, next to him
a Northern looking, pint of bitter man
"Ay lass, thou art al'rit", he does not say.
He reads his paper. Did he see her sway?

"Together, they live together,"
whispers in my head.
She is his wife, she shares his bed.
They do not look at each other
She stares straight ahead,

She knows I look, avoids my eyes.
They leave, he helps her down.
She does not hesitate or sway.
They walk together in their separate way.

THE CAYMANIAN ARTIST IN MANHATTAN

In this sea green dream of a painter's eerie
encased in your lofty nest you lie
your mind sprouting evergreen canvases.
Through your eyes and hands, iron shore
and sea grapes are defined.

Island spawned on casuarinas shaded shores.
You have taken no petal road but soared.
You lie in the seduction of the apple
casting your net wide, yet still adrift.

You catch the light spill
from paint punctured walls
silent, staccato birth of colour
invades and holds you enthralled.

Here the echoes are not faint
but crisp, clear intonations of
sharp, familiar melodies flowing
from lean, tapered fingers.

The sourdough concoctions of your mind
rise oven fresh each morning
to overflow on sunless canvases
which you must bring to life.

OLD CLICHE

He walks, wide wayward strides
black tracksuit, white striped trousers
the urban military uniform.
he walks wild and wide, hums a hip hop rhyme
has long since left, 'carry me ackee' rhythms
puts garage, house, the inevitable rap in his gait.

He's looking for that old cliché,
an African Queen
passes her each day in Brixton, Peckham,
Shepherd's Bush, but still can't find her.

EYE TO EYE

I must look out for your eyes
They injure me.
How my mind is scarred
by those chance, careless clashes
eye to eye.

Transience

TURN DOWN THE DAWN

Hold back the morning
I don't want to get up
turn down the dawn
switch off the sun
insist that the stars
continue to twinkle
stop the moon from escaping
gag the birds in the trees
freeze time
right now
today
I'm just
not
ready.

MORNING

Morning, guilty like an errant husband
steals quietly into this room
softly nudges colour out of the
grey and dark corners of a
fading night
tints with practised hand
each subtle hue
creates afresh our new day's life
meanders slowly through our waking mind
born again, renewed, one more time.

I'M SITTING HERE AWHILE

I'm sitting here awhile
because I've earned the right
to stop and wait to look
to watch the world go by.

Funny thing that
I've never done this before
funny thing, that
you might call me indolent,
a woman whose get up won't go

but I'm thinking, ruminating, chewing
on pieces of history trapped in my jaw.
I've worked hard all my life
this you should know

so I'm sitting here awhile
thinking about life
before it becomes
my time to go.

MORNING CHORES

I wrote a thousand poems in my mind this morning
But it was my time of day to clean and cook
The words came tumbling without much warning
Enough of them to fill an entire book.

And I in love with words waited
For the poems to take effect
Let them in, unchecked, unabated
And taken unawares did not suspect

That they would not submit to pen and paper
Would not return after my morning's labour
They disappeared, dissolved like vapour
And never again did they my mind favour.

CAYMAN SCHOOL DAY

Nothing exciting happened
on this clear bright day
except the children's
bursts of enthusiasm
my lunch
and the rain
when it came.

AFTERNOON CLASS

In this lazy day of quiet afternoon
the class sleeps
though they pretend to read
with heads bowed
the easy breath
flows gently
almost still
lashes flicker on soft cheeks
the door creaks
two friends converse
in low murmurs
breeze ruffles pages
and the children sleep.

TIME IS SHORT

Time is short
between
a bite
between
a slice
Life changes   Someone walks past.

Before the next sip of coffee
Before the next customer
The first perhaps the last
People walk past.

Real fur yesterday, fake today
between now and then
Someone   slipped consciousness
blood splattered bodies
We still walk past.

You stand in your space   she sits in hers
We watch you
We are watched
We all walk past.

A word   simple and small
could bring you into my world
A sentence could make you care
You and I know
We'll just walk past.

AMRYL

You heard Medusa calling,
   looked her in the eye,
      the point of no returning.

     You chose winter
       not waiting for the days
        when light grows longer,
         trapped seconds escaping.

     Soft winter, after the snowdrops
     would have been a better time,
     when rose bushes crack open
     their winter shells, stems unfurling.

You chose the gruff cadence
    of Dylan's voice while the
      rough embolism flowered,
        filling arteries, crawling,
        crawling.

    "Travelling is tiring,
   I'm not as young as I used to be,"
  rose to the tip of your tongue,
   then fell away as you were dying.

A JAR OF WORMS

Friends are hard to come by
and the test of friendship
grows more stringent every year.
School days of holding hands
playing games and chatting
quietly in corners are too soon over.

The greatest task then was to hold
a jar of worms for a boy cousin
who was considered friend
and fall immediately into that category
earmarked "women only."
Now friendship runs a deeper course
it is being careful, over cautious
then naked and vulnerable.

Friends used to be for laughter to
enjoy the moments which were
too good to be enjoyed alone
and friends were for protection
both yours and theirs.

The season has changed and
we are asking our friends to
share our sorrows and tell us truths
and we are no longer biting
our tongues when we feel anger
but we still like our friends.

Transience

It seems though that our friends
do not like our censure
even though we could accept theirs.

When the frontiers could be pushed
to more meaningful things we stop
and break apart, afraid to slide
out of control. Afraid to know
too much about each other.

LIKE WATER

You are in my thoughts
like water
One moment flood that
rushes through my brain
sweep through my senses
course through every vein
Then you desert me
trickle by a nerve
you tease and irk me
but dry's the valley's gorge.

NOT COFFEE SPOONS

My friend charts the passage of her life
through emotional landscapes
by what do I chart mine?

Not coffee spoons
no measures there for life.

Not idle hours
viewing dreams, asleep
on couch, in bed,
while the television transmits.

Not bookshelves filled with books
collected, read, unread.
Nor the aimless trawling walks
through shopping centres,
chic department stores,

another purchase made,
another meal prepared.

Not holidays
or endless racks of clothes.

Windows
have measured my circumstance.

Mine is a lifetime search for better windows
through which to view the world.

Not landscapes, or the view
they might afford.
It is the window that captivates and holds.

I am an inward, outward looking soul.
Look into my eyes
What sights do you behold?

BOB DYLAN SANG

For Amryl Johnson

Sitting on her couch she fell asleep.
her hands relaxed, face content
after Christmas, contemplating New Year.
Cards decorating the walls,
things to do, projects to begin and complete.
There was no warning. Just the usual winter flu,
no prior pulmonary heart attack.
She sat, waited patiently, but no one knew.

Bob Dylan sang a requiem lullaby,
one musical poet singing for another.
The neighbours didn't hear, didn't come.
'They weren't nice people,' someone later said.
'They couldn't care if you were alive or dead.'

Her suitcase standing in the hall
Post piling high on mat and wall
No heating kept her body cold
Frantic messages on the phone.
All we did was call and call.

CAYUGA LAKE

It snows on you tonight,
in the tumbleweed visceral avenues
of your night dreams.
The snow blows in from
Cayuga Lake and all the hollow
passages which gain entry
to our dappled lore.

A leaf falls as I read about
your snow and in that
transfixed splinter of time
I see fresh flakes
tumbling in the sleeping pause
of autumn's shedding leaves.

This simple gravity induced
compulsion of a leaf reveals
the password for our entry
into other times, another's soul.

So, standing in my mild, mellow
mist of autumn's golden gaze;
I feel the icy brush of snow
falling on Cayuga shores.

SICK DAY

The Kettle boils slowly today
Toast burned back is thrown away

Ginger jam, black coffee, honey stirred,
the sofa cushioned deep, begs me to stay

Invisible rain mists the spring garden
Heavy clouds, wind-whipped are blown away

The neighbour's cherry tree bows and nods
caught in a sudden gust the blossoms play

First slithery rays of sunshine stroke
the tall grass, while fever makes me sway.

WEST BAY LOVE SONG

When I gave you my love
it was a silent act
cushioned by night, and
pierced by the sound of the bull-frogs
calling their loves
after the rain had gone.
You gathered me whole, plucked cleanly,
And lost yourself in the only mystery -
Woman.

So I, being woman, foolishly
believed you were mine.
Now we sit in our silences
each in an individual pool.
There are no right words
to fill a silence like ours...

and now, when the rain falls
only my ears listen
the pillow comforts my fright
and the offspring of those
Long ago frogs
Croak under my window.

Now the smell that was you
that infused all my nights,

forgets to linger.
And when we meet
we never bridge the chasm.
We break down into this silence,
this silence
that goes deeper
than any act of love.

And I am faced at last
with the only mystery –
What does our silence say,
that our voices can not?

CARIBBEAN SUNSET FALLS

Darkness like the eyelids of a sleepy child descends
silencing tree top shy birds
stirring mosquitoes to singing life.
I had forgotten that the crickets sing
nature's lullaby at dusk
switched on without reminders
pitched and paced to slow
the beating of our hearts.

TIME FLIES

When did I last watch the sunset
glide smoothly across the skies
tint the whole world with colour?
I meant to every day, but time flies.

CAYMAN KAI LOVE SONG

Happy this day
as though it were fresh minted
sprung from within
creation of my being
here and now are my perspectives.
There is no circumstance
save this.
To feel you near,
to feel you near me,
ever, ever and a year.

NIGHT LINGERS

Light floated through an open doorway
elegant dust motes swirling in its path.
Light touched the tops of cherry trees,
grazed the ash-green underbelly of leaves
fluttering, celebrating a cool ripple of breeze.

Light glinted from the starry depths of fox eyes;
shone on wild canine paws, picking a delicate path
through night-muted air, swollen nectar ripe,
heavy with crushed flower perfumes.

Light highlighted the liquid silver trails
of ravenous snails, laying opalescent pearl eggs
clustered in mounds with no protective shells.
Light stroked the backs of beetles, colouring
their shells with midnight rainbow shades.

Light broke through sword thin slats in fences
threw criss-cross shadow patterns over grass,
swathed, the concrete sprouting paths,
undulating with unfulfilled spectral promises

Light chuckled and giggled, twirled and paraded.
When the sun shone light faded.

MELLIFLUOUS

Like moon pulled waves seeping into dry sand
lithe fingers fly, bending an immutable instrument
creating sounds blending into time.
Now sharp and hard, then soft, forlorn,
magic skimming spaces between sound and ear.
Mellifluous is where you are.

Sun echoes riffle desert sands and light night fires.
Flute music haunts the air awakens those who sleep,
frees an expansive breath. Opens hearts to
remembered cadences, rekindled, re-imagined riffs
floating free in diaphanous twilight dancing smoke.
Mellifluous is how we can become.

Mellow droplets spill fluid air tremors creating
wrap around ease. In this summer evening
notes fashion a filigree blend of longing,
looping strands across bruised midnight skies
melting into star spiked, sand dusted, darkness.
Where mellifluous, mellifluous, mellifluous lies.

Embrace

THE WALL

We strolled past your names
etched grey in black marble
an idea conceived by one
much the same in years, as you.

Young, Asian woman
like those you fought
with whom you died.
Life's wry irony
forces our acceptance.

This clear, clean idea
commemorates your muddy battles
nullifies the stench of your corpses
fades your psychedelic dreams
somehow delineates all lies
into the "old lie".
Yet, brings you back to life.

Reflected by your tomb
we descend into your names,
the first who died, stays first now always.
Here, at my feet, no yielding earth,
no gentle sway, or softening curve
straight
to the arrow's point
the boomerang's returned

Embrace

look up
look back
through
beyond
return

gaze in empty longing
to 1959
when you still stood, erect, supine
careless with the frailty of your youth.

Your thousand names blend into one.
For those who knew you
once stood, once fought
a man.

Now I stand
drowned, floundering
in the directory of your names
touched without touching

Only children feel, caress your names
they do not comprehend
for every name
once stood
a man
too young, too young
to understand.

The narrow path sun-bakes
our tears
which slide and hide in stone
as you once slid and hid
but, hide no more.

All that surrounds you
lies diminished.
To read or speak your name
we must see ourselves.

We stroll past the last known death
retrieve our shadows from the underworld
face those who are not named.
In banners, t-shirts, flags,
the war is up for sale
by aging veterans
who have yet to return
from "Nam"
Vietnam.

Embrace

TWELVE

I knew her when she was a child of twelve
Slender like young bamboo, her mind pliant papyrus reeds.
Skin pale, polished gold, a faint hint of cherry blossom on her cheeks
Her manner free of artifice, guileless seduction radiating from innocence.
I knew her when she was a child of twelve

Knew her like the smell of roasting chestnuts on hillside fires
The feel of sun-warmed skin in the palm of my hand
A child at play in palace courtyards, set on mountain tops
where frangipani, and honeysuckle fragranced winds hijinxed like children
in swift tumbling gusts;
Stray orphans forgotten in forbidden high-domed spaces.
I knew her when she was a child of twelve

Chose myself the red, or green-purple tinged sweet capsicum to make her
meals. Scattered edible petals of rare orchids to adorn a bed of white,
cinnamon scented rice.
Ordered juices to compliment the colours that she wore.
The orange of papaya, pale purple of passion fruit.

Dressed her in silk, that was my wish, that she should be draped in gold
trimmed sunset reds, strutting peacock blue and harem green.

I knew her when she was a child of twelve
when life was sunlight and amber shadows in the shade
and the rising sun scattered pomegranate coloured rays,

shimmering translucent in white morning light.

Beauty was this sunlight, wind-steered child.

So many years have passed. I gave her everything, gold, palaces, trips to foreign lands, a red Porsche, a helicopter just for her command.

I have simple pleasures now.
The smell of roasting chestnuts in the air.
A cup of coffee to begin my day, a smile, the fragrance of her hair.
I have grown old.

I hear the whispers floating through the palace walls.
She has gone. "Poor fool," they say. "Poor fool."
I sip the poisoned coffee unaware.

Today I miss the smell of roasting chestnuts in the air.
Where has the chestnut seller gone today?

[The wife of the King of Nepal was a twelve year old child when he married her. She ran away many years later with a chestnut seller after poisoning her husband.]

PEOPLE

The poppies are still blooming in November
seeds scattered
on the hind quarters of spring
lay dormant in early summer.

On silent reconnaissance
weakling shoots are encouraged
to scale the assault course
of rock and crumbling earth
break through the fine, baked
gauze of top-soil
to unfurl fledgling leaf
into the sun-scorched
desert air of our late summer.

These early recruits
wilting from heat exhaustion
encouraged others
sucking moisture from each other
then refused to grow further
shell-shocked, numb
until autumn rains
beat them down
left them awash in muddy soup trenches
numbed, humbled into homage
flattened where anchored.

Then sweet respite
foreign breezes
warmed the rain spiked air
suddenly fighting back, grew large
threw out shoots
confident, bold
flowered, blooming,
myriad coloured
fragile petals
dancing at the suggestion of a breeze

Poppies bloom in streets
of Streatham, Brixton, Peckham
All our world a Flanders field
In this November of poppies.

THE RETREAT

Even though he was world weary
he got up to go and get the books
which Cammy said he needed
to bring into this room, where the
light was better, especially in the
mornings, when the sun waking up
in the east filtered light through the trees
and the mist was retreating, to the edges
of the field, where in one corner
the cows had huddled together
sleeping standing up, which reminded
him of the students who told him about
cow tipping, which you do late
in the night, probably not to
get caught, and have angry farmers
coming after you because you've
knocked over their cows.
But that's all by the by
because she was more interested in looking
at the way the sun streamed into the room
and bounced it's reflection off the rich,
wood deep shine of the mahogany table
which he had polished, so long ago
before he arrived at the place
where he was too tired to care
and the world seemed an empty place

devoid of all meaning, and she knew he was
retreating like the mist, even though he
should be rising with the vapour which
rose early in the mornings from the
green algae covered pond which had
run clean and clear once, and if only he
would listen, could be like that again,
except his eyesight was failing and
increasingly he was always somewhere
else, never staying with the moment,
too worried about the future, when
futures never come and promises
are only half fulfilled, expectations
never met, and perhaps if he stared at
cows less and looked at himself more
and recognised the pleading that
stayed in her eyes, he would not
consider going, or worse,
permanently leaving.

PACING TIGERS

In the rise and fall of your chest
you will hear me
I am angry words
scattering themselves in the air around you,
scrabbling to reach the highest crescendos.
I have made voices scale peaks
beyond the heights of your imagination.
Each only asking, 'please hear me'.

Innocent puppy dogs chasing their tails,
unchecked, become tigers pacing in cages.
Believe me.

I am the space between
the cat's paw and the neck of the mouse,
the rock in your hand and a child's face,
the blade of a knife and his heart,
a bullet and a brain.
The chasm which marooned you in regret.

Like the bull elephant who sees a threat approaching
my ears flap forward
encompassing the perimeter of any space.
I am where red lives, agitating lives
be warned, I tell you when I am approaching.
I turn and you feel me dropping, subsiding, abating

a trick, to lull you into anticipating my demise
I have used it countless times.

Beware of the sudden gust of wind that inflates me.
I am majestic in full sail, if deadly.
Don't ignore me.

I am the momentum in your blood that drives you crazy.
Young men languish in prisons on my account,
I slice limbs, murder lives, kill friendships,
change history, because you pursue me.
I say again, believe me.
Don't challenge me.

Sentience

DON'T TALK TO ME OF LOVE

Don't talk to me of love, my heart knows.
Because morning lies broken at my feet,
sharp shards of dancing light, searching
for intimacy in a dump yard of broken promises.

Can we recycle lies and dreams?
We rein in pain, bind it tight
about our waists like children,
encumbered and enslaved, parents of sorrow.

Once we were sheltered by dreams,
those high arching layers of rainbows.
Colours now merged and mixed are sludge and mud.
Absence of light leaves only darkness.

We stumble in a night created
from dreams of rain reflected sunlight.
We can not find each other,
yet I am still here with you.

THOUSANDS MADE

Went fishing caught no fish but found a boy.

Pulled up half a black child's torso from the Thames
sans arms, elbows, hands, thighs, shins, sans foot or toes.
Without, without anything except shorts, red, popular make,
thousands sold. Like the boy, thousands made.

Spinning slowly this headless child,
swimming limbless in the Thames,
settling into the darkness of the mud.
Did his mother know? Did she cry?

Where are his fingers now?
Where buried are his silent lips?
Who rocked him when he could not sleep?

Went fishing, caught no fish but found a boy
Without arms, elbows, hands, thighs, shins.
Without anything except shorts, red, popular make,
thousands sold. Like the boy, thousands made.

CUBAN STORM

He rides his wooden wheeled boat,
"ship ahoy, ship ahoy"
sailing into a sudden thunderstorm
heading for silver flowing rivulets
a young Columbus discovering
a new land in the rain
in this transformed market place.

These are his water lands.
He stakes his claim;
as adults rush for cover
he heads for deserted open spaces
"un vela, un vela", "a sail, a sail."
He shouts and laughs,
splashing through his watery river road.

Sailing into tomorrow, like
Elian who rode life's bigger waves.
A mere pawn like this cherub sailor
dreaming of foreign lands
divided by oceans, while family bones
build a causeway for connection.

Drowning to reach better in the USA.
Everything is better in America,
more money, more food ... everything...

better, brighter, bigger in America.
Even better is better there than here.

Freedom and happiness are laughing boys
who know no better
ride the crest of river roads
while adults shelter from the thunderstorms,
green with the politics of longing and envy.

LITTLE MAN

Little man old and rubbed out,
shuffling to your door on stubborn feet
Bent, brittle, back,
beaten wet by torrential rain.
Little man,
the rain that falls on your poverty
falls also on mine.

I sit cocooned in my warm car
while you shuffle, wearily against nature.
The spotlight is now on you,
in it's beam I watch your progress.
In this dead of night I see you
walking towards your old wooden shack
the culmination of all your dreams.

Did you dream no further than here?
Did you make all those painful steps
all those emotional stumbles
to grope your way to a hammock
in a cluttered room?

You have arrived at a box
with galvanised roof that keeps the jungle at bay.
Your garden is soggy sand
and rain-waxed leaves.
Towering trees impartially drip
their burden on your cardboard back.

The jungle beats at your door
and you climb make-shift
breeze-block stairs
to your hammock bed.
Then swinging in your make-do heaven
you will contemplate the rain.
Your rain and mine.

LET MUSIC FLY

Play me a tune Keith
On the body of your flute
Through stops and starts
let your fingers descale that silver flying fish
Drop your notes like mercury
Let them slide off fish scales
Release the arpeggios drumming in your heat
Play me that music to die for rhythm
Pull it up through your spine
Stretch it out to reach mine
Play me that close your eyes
Reach into your belly
Driven by your seed
Procreation and need
Love and then die music
Smooth out the petals
Reach for the nectar
conjure up birds, lakes, forests
Spin webs for spiders
Make rivers cascade
let notes glide
Let sounds collide
Let breath and fingertips
Connive with flute and lips
Let music fly
Reawaken memories

Don't let them die Keith
Don't let them die
Squeeze sound from your lips
Let the music feed mine
Drip honey notes and fill me
Let your moist breath slide down
Warm up cold metal
Play music to love and die for
Play music to move me.

GREEN MOON

My green moon went to sleep
leaving me riding the night sky.
Revealing the traces of it's shadows
on my brow, hiding in the spaces
between pauses and full stops.

I danced our troubles away.
For I was young then, unfragmented,
collecting stars with my eyes,
weaving ancient rhythms into my dreams,
catching moonlight on my tongue.

Wrapped in the youth of my sea green games,
searching for meaning in the sound of names.
Not any more, not any more.
I cannot play now.

BACK HOME

In the dark, the shadows
fall like rain
the walls breathe out
the insects stop
the room sits bated-breath
and all stands still, inanimate
The night time,
when breathing slows to nil.

END SONG

Is there a song
that isn't about love?
This poem must end now,
before it becomes one.

............and ......

the words came

tumbling without much warning

Enough of them to fill an entire book.

Embrace

ACKNOWLEDGEMENTS

The following poems have been published previously as indicated:

The Way We Were (2000) **IC3, The Penguin Book of New Black Writing in Britain;** *West Bay Love Song* (1993) **Mating Rituals,** Poetry Now

Fresh Mornings (1995) **Poets of the 90's,** Arrival Press

Let Music Fly (1996) **Poetry Magic,** Anchor Press

My Grandmother Sings to Me, Sun Gods, Someone Else, Snow Queen, **Her Mind's Eye,** Pyramid Press

Sun Gods, My Grandmother Sings to Me, **Voice Memory Ashes,** Mango Publishing

Sun Gods, My Grandmother Sings to Me, Polished Silver, **MaComere vol. 1 (Journal)**

A Farewell Song, **MaComere vol. 4** (Journal)

Food File, Turn Down the Dawn (Nov. 1995 to Jun 1996) **Poetry on the Buses**

Let Music Fly (1996) **Poems on Walls**

FORTHCOMING TITLES

MAKING TIME TO CATCH A RHYME by LENNOX CARTY (children) ISBN 0 904 521 62 1

NEW EDITION

THE GROUNDINGS WITH MY BROTHERS by WALTER RODNEY (non-fiction) ISBN 0 904 521   57 5

RECENTLY PUBLISHED

JOURNEY TO AN ILLUSION: The West Indian in Britain by DONALD HINDS (non-fiction) ISBN 0 904 521   25 7

THE FEAST OF THE NINE VIRGINS by JAMEELA SIDDIQI (fiction) ISBN 0 904 521 29 4

ALREADY PUBLISHED

JOURNEY AS THE WIRE BEND: UP RIVER WHERE THE STORY END by Lisa Levi (Suitable for all ages) ISBN 0 904 521 516

IN THE BORDER COUNTRY AND OTHER STORIES by Andrew Salkey (fiction) ISBN 0 904 521   94 X

IN THE TRICKSTER TRADITION: The Novels of Andrew Salkey, Francis Ebejar and Ishmael Reed (fiction)   ISBN 0 904 521   97 4

ANANCY,TRAVELLER by ANDREW SALKEY (fiction) ISBN 0 904 521 85 0

ANANCY'S SCORE by ANDREW SALKEY ISBN 0 950 154 68 7

CARIBBEAN FOLK TALES AND LEGENDS compiled and edited by ANDREW SALKEY ISBN 0 904 521 17 6

BOOKS AVAILABLE FROM:
BOGLE L'OUVERTURE PRESS

PO.BOX 2189, LONDON W13 0ZQ